Children *of the* Bible

BROWNLOW PUBLISHING COMPANY, INC.
6309 Airport Freeway, Fort Worth, Texas 76117

Children
of the
Bible

26 Exciting Bible Stories About Children of the Bible

by

Cindy Baw and Paul C. Brownlow

Illustrated by

James Seward/Creative Studios I

BROWNLOW PUBLISHING COMPANY, INC.

FORT WORTH, TEXAS

Grateful appreciation is expressed to
Alice Brown and Pat Kirk
for their careful reviews and
evaluations of this book

Contents

I. *Introductory Poem* 8

II. *Children of the Old Testament* 9

   1. The Story of Isaac 10

   2. The Story of Ishmael 12

   3. The Story of Joseph 16

   4. The Story of Miriam 20

   5. The Story of Moses 24

   6. The Boy Who Led a Blind Man 26

   7. The Story of Samuel 30

   8. The Story of David 34

   9. The Story of Mephibosheth 38

  10. The Widow's Son 42

  11. The Young Lads 46

  12. Two Boys Saved from Slavery 48

  13. The Shunammite Boy 52

  14. The Little Slave Girl 56

  15. The Story of King Josiah 60

  16. The Story of King Joash 64

III. *Children of the New Testament* 67

   1. The Birth of Jesus 68

   2. Jesus as a Boy 72

   3. The Nobleman's Son 74

   4. The Daughter of Jairus 76

   5. The Boy with the Loaves and Fish 78

   6. The Little Sick Boy 82

   7. The Story of Rhoda 84

   8. Paul's Nephew 88

   9. The Story of Timothy 90

  10. Jesus and the Children 94

IV. *Concluding Poem* 96

Children *of the* Bible

The children of the Bible,
  I love to read their story,
I learn about the Bible,
  I learn about God's glory.

There's Miriam . . . and Moses . . .
  And little Samuel, too . . .
And Rhoda and Timothy . . .
  And Jesus was a child, too!

The children of the Bible,
  How I'd love to know each one,
To know what they liked to eat,
  And the games they played for fun.

For now, I'll only see them
  In the pages of this book.
So let's begin and hurry,
  I can't wait to take a look!

*Children
of the
Old Testament*

Do you know anyone who is a hundred years old? That may seem very, very old to you. But that is exactly how old Abraham was when God gave him another son, Isaac. No wonder they called the baby Isaac, because the name means "laughter." Abraham laughed with great joy when God promised him a son. Sarah laughed because she just could not believe it would be possible for her to have a child when she was ninety years old. But nothing is too hard for God.

Yes, Isaac was a very special child who was taught to love and trust God. As Isaac grew up, he and his father Abraham had good times together. They fixed tents, took care of the sheep, and probably played some Hebrew sports together. Just as your parents are so very proud of you, Isaac's parents were lovingly proud of him.

But suddenly all of their family happiness turned to sadness. For the Lord told Abraham, "Take your son Isaac to the land of Moriah, and offer him there as a burnt offering." No doubt Abraham was saying in his heart, "Why God? Why command that our son be offered as a burnt offering? He is our special child and joy in old age. Now why kill him? Why offer him as a sacrifice? There are plenty of lambs we can offer." There was no way Abraham could know why God gave this command. He just had to believe that God would bring good out of what looked so bad. Even though Abraham could not understand why God would ask such a thing, he trusted God completely and made plans to obey.

But remember, Isaac did not know about the strange request God made of his father. He obediently traveled with his father to the mountain where the sacrifice was to be made. As Isaac talked about many things, he curiously asked his father, "Where is the lamb for the burnt offering?" Do you think Isaac might have been afraid if he had known that he was the one to be offered instead of a lamb?

Never doubting what God said, Abraham built the altar after they arrived at the mountain. The Bible tells us that Abraham "arranged the wood, and bound his son Isaac, and laid him on top of the wood . . . and took the knife to kill his son." The most unusual thing of all is that Isaac did not say a word or complain at all. He obeyed his father, even if the result was death. That took a strong faith and a complete obedience.

Suddenly — like a flash — God stopped the whole event. "Stop," God said. "Now I know for sure that you really love me, since you were willing to give up what you love most for me. There is a ram caught by his horns in a bush nearby. Offer it instead of your son."

What an experience! God had fully tested the faith of this father and son. And they passed the test. They didn't understand why God gave this command. But they knew God had ordered it. And that was enough. So they did it and God did bring good out of bad. Then they could be glad they had obeyed God, hug each other, and thank God and praise His name.

Prayer Thought: Help me to obey, Lord, without complaining and asking "Why?"

Let's Talk About the Story:

1. Did Abraham understand God's request to offer Isaac as a burnt offering?
2. Explain how Abraham and Isaac obeyed.
3. Why do you think that Isaac was such a special son to Abraham?

Isaac

God told Abraham to give his son.
  Abraham cried,
  But said, "It is done."

Isaac obeyed and became the lamb.
  God said, "Wait,
  I'll send you a ram."

THE STORY OF ISHMAEL

Have you ever heard about the boy who grew up to be called a "donkey man?" Now, he did not look like a donkey. He was called "donkey" because he was rough and wild.

The boy's name was Ishmael.

His father was a very rich and important man named Abraham. His mother was the household maid or servant in Abraham's family. Her name was Hagar. She was from another country — Egypt.

When Ishmael was fourteen years old, a baby boy was born into the family. He was called Isaac and his mother's name was Sarah. While the boys had the same father, Abraham, they had different mothers. This means they were half-brothers.

Genesis 16:1-13; 21:1-20

As you see, all of a sudden Ishmael was no longer the center of attention. Baby Isaac was now the center of attention. And that's the way it should be, for a baby can't do anything for himself. But, still Ishmael became envious.

Perhaps you know how Ishmael felt. You may have a baby at your house now and feel a little left out and envious. If so, you may have forgotten how much time it takes to care for a tiny baby. This is because you are no longer a small baby. You can do many things by yourself now.

Well, Ishmael's envy got him in trouble. It always does.

When the baby Isaac became a toddler, their father gave a big feast celebrating his growth. "What a beautiful child Isaac is," a party guest gooed. "Why he looks just like his father!" Ishmael wondered why no one even seemed to notice that he was alive. He wanted attention so badly! What could he do to make people pay attention to him, too? Ishmael was so envious that he mocked Isaac and made fun of him. This made Isaac's mother, Sarah, very angry. She became so angry that she told Abraham to send Ishmael and his mother away. She didn't want that older boy growing up and making fun of her baby boy. She said, "Send Hagar and her boy away, for they are troublemakers."

This bothered Abraham. It made him sad for trouble to come into his family. For he was a good and kind man and loved them all. He hardly knew what to do.

At this point, the Lord spoke to Abraham: "Don't be troubled about Ishmael and his mother. Do as Sarah has requested and send them away. This will help my plans for both boys. Isaac is to inherit and receive everything that is yours, and from his children a strong nation of people will be formed. But I, the Lord, will also take care of Ishmael, and from his children another great nation of people will come forth."

The next morning, comforted by the Lord's promise, Abraham told Hagar and Ishmael that they must go away. So he gave them bread and a bottle of water for the journey. Abraham expected them to return to Egypt, the land from which Hagar had come.

But on the way Hagar got lost in the desert. There they were in a hot, sandy desert, lost and helpless. They were tired and thirsty, and the water was all gone. The hot sun baked Ishmael's lips and burned his skin, and there was no water to satisfy his thirst.

Hagar and Ishmael were both frightened. "We'll die here in this desert," they thought. The mother could not bear to see the boy die of thirst. So she placed him under a bush to give him a little protection from the sun and went away.

And just at the worst time when the mother was crying and the boy moaning for water, she heard a voice that said to her: "What troubles you, Hagar? Fear not. God heard you and the boy."

It was the voice of an angel. God had not forgotten them. Hagar looked and a bubbling well of water was near by.

Isn't it encouraging to know that God can give us more than we think? He gave them more than just a drink, He gave them a whole well!

After this difficult experience, Hagar decided not to go to Egypt. She made her home in the desert where God had given them a well. There in the desert, Ishmael grew up, far away from the big crowds. The land was open and he was free to run all over it as a boy of the outdoors. He grew strong in his arms and learned to shoot with the bow and arrow. He was a wild man — a "donkey man." But it was a wild, harsh country.

And God did keep His promise. Ishmael did become the father of a strong people. His children were rough and wild like him, and lived and wandered in the desert just as he had done.

Prayer Thought: Lord, help me to be satisfied with all you have given me. I do not want to envy others.

Let's Talk About the Story:

1. Which animal was used to describe Ishmael?
2. How were Ishmael and Isaac half-brothers?
3. Why was Ishmael envious of Isaac?
4. What did Sarah do after Ishmael "mocked" Isaac?
5. Can you think of a time when you were envious?

Ishmael

Ishmael laughed and made fun,
    Then they put him on the run.
God protected him I tell,
    Sent an angel and a well.

THE STORY OF JOSEPH

Have you ever dreamed that something wonderful happened to you? Perhaps you dreamed that you were rich and famous. Well, that was exactly what a boy named Joseph dreamed. Joseph was one of the twelve sons of Jacob. And he was so eager to share his dreams with his eleven brothers that he quickly asked them, "Guess what I dreamed last night?"

Now Joseph's brothers were already jealous of Joseph. They knew he was their father's favorite son. Since jealousy brings out the meanness in people, his brothers were very hateful as Joseph excitedly related his dreams. Even though his brothers were not very anxious to hear, Joseph told them anyway.

"Last night I dreamed we were harvesting our wheat crop. Each of us tied our own stack of wheat into a bundle. When we finished, my bundle stood straight up. But your bundles marched up and bowed down to mine."

This dream angered his brothers. They asked Joseph, "Are you really going to rule over us?" The Bible tells us that "they hated him even more for his dreams and for his words." Now if you had been Joseph, would you have gotten the message to keep your dreams to yourself? Probably not and neither did Joseph.

Joseph eagerly told his brothers another dream. "In my dream," Joseph spoke, "the sun and moon and eleven stars bowed down to me." This made his brothers even more jealous of him. They didn't like little brother's dreams. They growled to themselves, "What a little bragger! We might have to teach him a lesson!"

Think of a time when you were jealous of a brother, sister, or a friend. Perhaps you even had the foolish idea that your parents loved your brother and sister more than they loved you. Maybe you became so jealous that you got angry and yelled, hit, or told a lie. Jealousy makes a person "crazy" — he or she simply cannot think clearly.

Unless jealousy is overcome, it will get uglier and meaner. It affected Joseph's brothers that way. When they saw Joseph wearing the beautiful coat of many colors their father had given him, their jealousy caused them to do an awful thing. They stripped Joseph of his pretty coat and threw him into a pit to die.

About this time, some merchants came by on their way to Egypt — another country. The brothers asked themselves, "Why should we kill Joseph? We can get rid of him and make some money at the same time!" So they sold Joseph as a slave and he was taken to Egypt. There Joseph later would do hard work without any pay. He would also be sent to prison even though he had done nothing wrong.

Do you know what else those mean brothers did? They took Joseph's coat and dipped it in goat's blood, and took it back to their father. They tricked their old father into thinking his younger son Joseph had been killed by a lion or a bear. They told him, "We found this coat outside. We don't know if it belongs to your son or not." Jacob sobbed, "I will cry about Joseph every day until I die."

This shows how one bad thing leads to another one. At first, the brothers were jealous. Then they hated; then they lied. The brothers also had to live every day afraid that someone would find out what they had done.

But what an amazing success story for Joseph! Through all of the suffering and bad events in Joseph's life, Joseph believed in God. And God made everything work together for good. God doesn't always follow our time schedule. But God always brings good out of bad for those who trust him.

Years later, Joseph became an important ruler in Egypt. He was in charge of collecting and selling all the food. Now there was no food in Canaan, where Joseph's brothers lived. Jacob, their father, told them, "We will die if you don't buy food in Egypt where there is plenty." The brothers came to Egypt desperate for food. Guess what? The brothers did not even recognize Joseph when they came to him to buy food. But Joseph knew his brothers immediately!

Remember the dream? Now Joseph's dream came true. The brothers did come and bow down before him. Joseph tested his brothers to find out how they treated one another. He found they were now kind and protected each other. Then what do you think he did? You are probably thinking that they should be punished. Maybe they should be allowed to starve to death or perhaps even be put in prison.

But Joseph was God's young man, and he forgave his brothers. Not only did Joseph forgive his brothers, but he gave them "the best of the land." He gave them wagons, clothes, silver, donkeys, food, and more food. The Bible tells us that Joseph kissed all his brothers and cried tears of joy at being able to see them again. What a wonderful example! Joseph forgave his brothers — whether or not they deserved to be forgiven.

Joseph knew that God had used him to save many people from starving. What had looked like a curse when Joseph was a slave, turned out to be a blessing. God blessed all of Joseph's family, and especially Joseph.

Prayer Thought: Lord, help me to forgive those who hurt me.

Let's Talk About the Story:

1. Why did Joseph's brothers hate him? Was it Joseph's fault at all?
2. Pretend you were one of Joseph's brothers. How would you have treated Joseph?
3. When you do something wrong, how do you feel on the inside?
4. If a friend, brother, or sister hit you, told a lie about you or argued with you, what should you do?

Joseph

Joseph had a pretty coat,
  It made his brothers mad.
They sold him into slavery,
  And lied to their dad.

Joseph was sent to Egypt,
  Became a mighty man;
Forgave his brothers' evil deed,
  And fed them from the land.

Exodus 1:1-2:10

Can you remember an unusual time of joy when God sent a new baby to your house or to a friend's house? If so, then you can understand the happiness that came to a young girl named Miriam. When she was twelve years old, a beautiful baby boy was born into her family. Isn't that exciting? Now she was a big sister with a baby brother. Now she was needed more than ever to help her mother. She could be the babysitter.

But not all was well! The old mean king of Egypt named Pharoah had ordered all Hebrew baby boys to be thrown into the Nile River. Why would he do this bad thing? He was afraid. He was afraid that if he let the baby boys live, he might lose his control over the Hebrew people. They were his slaves. He thought that the Hebrew people might become too strong for him to rule. The slaves might tell him that they were not going to take his cruel treatment any longer. They might tell him they were going to be free people and not slaves. So, wanting to keep them weak and afraid, he decided to kill all the baby boys. He was thinking only of himself. Selfishness always causes trouble.

As you can see, the mother whose name was Jochebed, and the sister, Miriam, had a problem. What could they do to keep the Egyptians from getting that baby boy and drowning him in the river? For three

months they hid him. But every day it became more dangerous. He was getting bigger and "noisier."

Something else had to be done! What could they do? They made a basket, a little boat out of reed-like plants. Then they spread tar on the outside of the basket boat to keep water from leaking into it. To make it more comfortable for their baby, they lined it with cloths.

Now came the hardest part of all. Miriam and her mother took the basket and the baby down to the river. They put the baby in the basket and set it in the water at the edge of the river. Oh, how they must have prayed for the baby's safety.

As the mother returned home, she said to the big sister Miriam, "Watch him and see what happens."

It was not long until King Pharoah's daughter came with her servants to bathe in the river. The princess saw the basket and ordered a servant to bring it to her. When she opened the lid, she got a surprise. There was a baby, a crying baby, and she felt sorry for him.

"What a beautiful baby! I'll keep him for my own child. I'll name him Moses because I picked him up out of the water."

Miriam had been paying very close attention to all this. She then came running to the princess and said, "Would you like for me to get a nurse of the Hebrew women to care for the child?"

The princess said, "Yes, please do."

So the sweet and watchful Miriam rushed away and brought back the baby's own mother. But she didn't tell the princess that the nurse was the baby's mother. That was a secret.

The princess was well pleased and said to the mother, "Take the child and nurse it for me, and I will pay you." When the baby got older, he was taken back to the princess, Pharoah's daughter.

So the boy grew up in the king's palace. No one could harm him there. Everyone was nice to him and treated him as if he were the king's grandson.

Little baby Moses grew up to become powerful and famous. Later he led God's people out of their slavery and away from the cruel treatment they had suffered under the rule of Pharoah and the Egyptians.

What a thrilling story! And all of it made possible because of the love, bravery and kindness of an older sister. Miriam did her part.

Do you have any younger brothers or sisters? If so, you can show special attention to them, just as Miriam did. But even if you don't have any brothers or sisters, you can still show special attention to other people.

Prayer Thought: Help me to be attentive to the needs of other people around me that I can help — especially those in my own home.

Let's Talk About the Story:

1. Why was Miriam's brother not safe at home?
2. How was Miriam a good sister?
3. Name a time this week when someone paid special "attention" to you. How did you feel?
4. Name a time this week when you were attentive to your parents, sister, brother, or a special friend.

Miriam

Into the river she put him,
  But not for a bath or a swim.
She hoped the princess would find him,
  And take him to the palace as kin.

THE STORY OF MOSES

Remember the story about the big sister Miriam who looked after her baby brother Moses? Remember how God worked through a brave mother, an attentive sister and a kind princess to save little Moses?

Moses' mother, Jochebed, loved him very much. She was the one who hid Moses. She had made the basket boat that floated Moses safely to the arms of the bathing princess.

Miriam had made sure that the basket really was safe for sleeping baby Moses. When Moses had floated to the princess, Miriam was there just in time. She offered to help the princess find a nurse for Moses. Miriam then ran to get her mother who was selected as the nurse.

And what about the princess? When she found the baby Moses, she knew he was one of the Israelite babies that Pharoah wanted to destroy. But she didn't care about the king's foolish rules! She saw the beautiful and helpless baby and knew he needed a safe home. She took him to be her very own adopted son to grow up as a rich boy in a beautiful palace!

A Life of Service

Yes, God used Moses' mother and his big sister and the princess of Egypt in a special way. God used each of them to save Moses and to save God's people from slavery. God had a special plan of service for Moses, just as He has a plan for your life, too!

What would happen to Moses in Egypt? What would God do for him next? Since Moses was the son of the princess, he was taught by the very best teachers in Egypt. They taught him reading, writing, arithmetic, medicine, history, science, law and all subjects. He learned about many things. You see, part of God's plan was for Moses to learn from the best teachers in Egypt. God was getting him ready for service. In the same way God wants you to do your best and learn from the Sunday School and school teachers He provides for you.

So the baby taken from the water grew into one of the most important men of all times. He served God by becoming the leader of God's people. He led them out of the cruel slavery forced on them by that mean king. We never can tell what a great person a baby may become.

When Moses was playing with his school friends, he never imagined that God would use him to work miracles and free people from slavery. Every day you play with your friends or learn at school. But can you imagine the wonderful and extra special plans God has for your future? He is working through the people and events in your life. He wants to train you to do great and wonderful things in His service. Are you ever unhappy because things are not going as you would like? Sometimes do you not get what you want? Is a friend selfish or fussy? Are you made to work? Do you think your parents are too strict? Well, thank God for the special person He is making of you. All of this is a part of your training for service.

Prayer Thought: Thank you for my parents, my friends, my teachers, and the way you are using what happens to me. Shape me into a very special person of service you can use.

Let's Talk About the Story:

1. Who was Moses' big sister?
2. Who found Moses in the river?
3. How could God use school and learning in your life?
4. Remember, right now the Lord has a very special plan of service for your life. Do you have any idea what that plan might be?

Moses

Moses was a good little boy
  Full of life and full of joy.
God had plans for the boy to fill.
  And Moses tried to do God's will.

Have you ever had the chance to help a blind boy or girl?

This is a story about kindness. It is the story of a young boy who helped a blind man. The man's name was Samson. Perhaps you remember that he was the strongest man who ever lived. We don't know the boy's name, but that doesn't matter. It's what he was and what he did that really counts.

Yes, children are important to God. He has plans for each one. Samson was chosen by God to be a hero of his people before he was ever born. God sent His angel to Samson's parents-to-be with a very exciting announcement. The angel said, "No razor may be used to cut his hair, for the boy is set apart to God. He will begin God's work of saving His people from the Philistines." The Philistines were enemies of God's people. After telling this thrilling news to the childless couple, the angel went back up to heaven in a flame of fire.

Soon Samson was born as the angel promised. As Samson grew, like all healthy children do, the Lord blessed him. Samson knew that he had special strength and a special job to do for God and His people. He understood that he must never cut his hair or tell the secret of his strength.

Samson grew into manhood. He chose a beautiful Philistine woman named Delilah to be his girlfriend. He wanted to trust her and to share his heartfelt dreams with her. But Delilah loved money more than she did Samson. Her own people paid her to find out the secret of Samson's strength. Day after day Delilah begged Samson, "If you really loved me, you would trust me with the secret of your strength." At first Samson teased her about the secret. He even gave her three wrong answers. Each time, she tested him and found out that he had tricked her.

But one day, when he was sick and tired of her constant begging, Samson told her the truth. She, in turn, told the secret to her own people. Later when they were alone together, Delilah had Samson to sleep with his head on her lap. She then called a barber to cut off his hair while he slept. Snip, snip, snip! Off fell the seven braids of Samson's hair to the floor! Then she called, "Samson, the Philistines are here to capture you!" Samson awoke thinking that he could use his strength to get free, but his strength had left him!

Judges 13:1-24; 16:1-30

The cruel Philistines grabbed him, punched out his eyes and put him in metal chains. Then they made Samson a slave in the prison grinding out wheat. Day after day, Samson walked around in circles pushing a heavy mill wheel, crushing the wheat beneath his feet. What a sad life for a handsome hero!

Later, the Philistines had a big party to celebrate their capture of Samson. "Dagon, our god, has given Samson over to us," they cheered. They then had a great idea for some fun. Why not bring Samson out like a clown to entertain the party guests? "Where is your strength now, Samson?" they teased him. They did not notice that Samson's hair had been growing out again.

Right here is where the unnamed boy comes into the story. The Bible just calls him a boy. Samson called the servant boy to him, saying, "Put me where I can feel the pillars that support the temple. Then I can rest against them." The boy felt sorry for Samson. He wanted to help him. So the boy led him to the right place.

Samson prayed to God to give him strength just once more and to let him die along with the Philistine rulers.

God answered Samson's prayer. As Samson pushed the pillars on each side of him, he felt strength exploding within him. He pushed with all of his strength. The temple to a false god fell down with a mighty crash!

Samson and many of the Philistines died, but his job for God was done. The young servant boy had played an important part in bringing about God's will.

Who knows what can happen when children and adults alike show even small acts of kindness to others. Great things for God may be the result!

Prayer Thought: Lord, show me someone to be kind to each day.

Let's Talk About the Story:

1. What secret did Samson tell Delilah?
2. How did the boy show kindness to Samson?
3. What did Samson do before he pushed the columns down?
4. How can you show kindness this week? Name the person and the way you will show kindness.

The Boy Who Led a Blind Man

Samson was strong, Samson was brave;
  God's people he was sent to save.
But Samson put a woman's love
  Between him and his God above;
Then a kind boy of the land
  Led blind Samson by the hand!

Can you think of a holiday in May that honors a person who is very important in your life? She is the person who cooks your food, washes your clothes, and keeps your home neat and clean. She is your friend and helper who loves you in a very special way. Who is this woman? You are right. She is your own mother! And her special May holiday is Mother's Day.

Mothers love their children. They enjoy taking care of them. Some women want to be mothers very much, but they have no child to love and to care for.

Hannah was a woman who had no children. She wanted a baby so much that she became very unhappy. Her husband told her, "I love you, Hannah. Isn't my love enough to make you happy?" One heartless mother even made fun of Hannah. "Too bad that you don't have a child of your own like the rest of us," she teased. Hannah was heartbroken! Tears rolled down her cheeks! What she wanted most — a son— she did not have.

Wasn't she a woman who loved and served God? Why not ask God for a son? He was the only one who could help her. He alone understood how she felt! Hannah went to the temple. She prayed, "Dear Lord, if you will give me a son, I will give him back to you." Hannah dried her eyes. She was happy for she trusted God with her life.

God said "yes" to Hannah. Her son, Samuel, was born. "I asked God for you," she told little Samuel often as he grew. "One day soon, back to God you shall go. For I have promised to give you to Him."

That day came rather quickly for Hannah. Time seems to pass very fast for mothers as they watch their children grow up. One day Hannah said, "Samuel, the time has come for you to live with Eli the priest at the temple in Shiloh. I have taught you about God. Eli will teach you even more about Him. I will pray for you every day while we are apart. Each year I will come to visit you."

So Samuel went to live in the temple. Eli taught him many things, just as his mother had said. Eli was kind, too, just like an adopted grandfather.

While Samuel was living in God's house with Eli the priest, a very interesting thing happened! To better understand it, pretend that you are sound asleep and suddenly a loud voice wakes you up. This is what happened to Samuel. He heard a voice that called, "Samuel! Samuel!"

"Here I am," said Samuel. He jumped out of bed and ran to the old priest, Eli. He was obedient and helpful even if it was the middle of the night.

Much to Samuel's surprise, Eli said, "I didn't call you. Go lie down again."

So, probably thinking he was dreaming things, he went back to bed. But once again he heard a voice saying, "Samuel! Samuel!"

Now this time Samuel knew that Eli must be teasing him so he ran to Eli again and said, "Here I am sir, since you called me."

"I did not call you, my son," said Eli. "Go and lie down again."

The Boy Who Listened

This happened three times, and the last time Eli knew it was the Lord who was speaking to Samuel. So Eli wisely told Samuel, "If the Lord calls again, say, 'Speak, Lord, for your servant is listening.' "

After losing a lot of sleep Samuel went back to bed with "listening" ears. So the next time when the Lord called, the boy said, "Speak, Lord, for your servant is listening."

What did the Lord have to say? Surely it would be something very important. "I am going to say something that will make everyone's ears tingle," declared the Lord.

God told Samuel about His plans for God's people in the future. Samuel would become an important part of those plans. He would become a prophet, preacher, teacher, and judge for the people of Israel. He would even crown kings and teach them how to be God's rulers. And he started learning how to be a great leader when he was still a boy!

Do you listen to your parents and teachers to learn all that you can? If you do, you will be ready as you grow up to share what you know with others. You will be useful in God's work — just like Samuel!

Prayer Thought: Lord, help me to listen to you and to those people you have placed over me to protect me.

Let's Talk About the Story:

1. Why was Hannah sad?
2. Who was calling Samuel in the middle of the night?
3. Why is it important for children to listen to their parents?
4. How do we listen to God today?

Samuel

"Samuel, Samuel,"
The sleeping boy heard
And three times to Eli he ran.

So the next time he listened
And heard God's Word.
God told him, "You'll be a great man."

How many brothers or sisters do you have? Do you have as many as seven? David had seven handsome brothers in his family. He was the youngest son and still lived with his father in Bethlehem.

Three of David's brothers were away from home fighting in King Saul's army. David was left at home to take care of his father's sheep. David did not seem to mind staying at home with his sheep. In fact, at times being a shepherd was just as dangerous as being in the army.

One day while David was watching his sheep nibble tender green grass, he saw a scary sight. A hungry bear came out from a clump of bushes looking for a free, easy meal — a careless sheep. The bear had very sharp teeth and powerful paws which could destroy a sheep or a boy in seconds. Would David hide from the bear? Would he run away? After all, if the bear ate one helpless sheep, David would still have plenty of other sheep left. But David sprang into action. He killed the bear and saved all his sheep.

. Another time, David saved his sheep from a hungry lion that attacked his flock. David was not afraid of bears or lions. He trusted God to protect both him and his flock.

Some days everything around David was peaceful. The green pastures were covered with happy, nibbling sheep. David would look at the clouds, the hills, the sun, and wildflowers around him. He loved God and often sang, "The Lord is my shepherd," as he watched his sheep.

One day David's father sent him to do an important job. "David," he said, "I am wor-

ried about your brothers in the army. I have not heard from them lately. Please take these ten loaves of bread and ten cheeses to the hungry soldiers. See if your brothers are safe."

David was happy to go. He took the bread and cheese and started out to look for his brothers' army camp. Was he ever surprised when he found Saul's army! The big, strong army men were hiding in the rocks and mountains nearby. They were so scared that they weren't even ashamed to run away from their Philistine enemies. The Philistines were playing a dangerous game with God's people, the Israelites. Each day they would send out a huge giant named

A Boy of Courage

Goliath. He was nine feet and four inches tall. He was covered from head to toe with heavy spiked armor. He carried a sword and shield. Every day he would tromp out and bellow like thunder, "Send one of your men out here to fight me!" He would then make fun of God and His puny, scared army.

When David saw this pitiful scene, he was furious at Goliath. David fumed, "Who does he think he is that he can make fun of God? I will fight him."

David's brothers were mad at him. They thought that little brother had just tagged along to spy on them. They were also probably ashamed. They were too afraid to fight Goliath and so was the rest of the army!

King Saul found out that David, the young shepherd boy, had the courage to fight the fearless Goliath. David was the only one who even dared to think about it. He was not the slightest bit scared. He seemed to know that he would win against the giant. David told King Saul, "God helped me kill a bear and a lion that attacked my sheep. He will give me this giant Philistine also!"

King Saul was worried about David. But what could he do but let him go? Saul gave David his armor, but it was too heavy and bulky for a shepherd boy. David was used to the freedom of moving constantly with sheep. David wouldn't need it, anyway. God was his strength and protector.

David went out to fight the huge giant with a little sling shot and five smooth stones. When Goliath saw him, he couldn't believe his eyes. Could Israel's hero be a young, untrained boy armed only with rocks and a sling! Goliath roared to David, "I'll feed you to the birds."

David answered peacefully, "You come to me with a sword and spear. I come to you in the name of the Lord you have dishonored. He will give you over to me."

David swung his arm around and around. He let go of his sling. The well-aimed rock flew through the air and struck Goliath on his huge head. Goliath fell down with a crash. He never got up again. Israel cheered! The Philistine army ran away. The scared people of God came out of their hiding places and chased after the fleeing army. God's people were saved!

God had won a great victory and had used a brave boy to do it. God could not use the scared soldiers. But God could use the brave boy who loved and trusted Him to win a battle against a huge bully.

Does a brave child who trusts God live at your house? Believing in God will make you have courage. Then you will be able to do things that might scare other people who don't know God. Believe, trust, win!

Prayer Thought: Lord, help me to trust in you and to have courage.

Let's Talk About the Story:

1. What special work did David do at home?
2. Why did David go to the battlefield?
3. What did the giant say he would do to David?
4. Why was David unafraid?
5. Where does courage come from?

David

Big Goliath was a bully,
  He loved to shout and call.
But David with a little rock
  Made big Goliath fall.

THE STORY OF MEPHIBOSHETH

A terrible accident happened to a little five year old prince named Mephibosheth. We think princes and princesses are very special. They live in beautiful palaces and have lots of toys. They even have a nurse who plays with them and takes care of them. But princes and princesses have their troubles like everyone else. They are human and if they fall, they get hurt just as we do.

One day a messenger came running to Mephibosheth's house with some very sad news, "Our soldiers lost the battle! Both the prince's father and grandfather were killed. Run for your lives to a safe place." The frightened nurse grabbed Mephibosheth quickly, carrying him in her arms. But as she ran, he slipped from her grasp. As he fell, his little feet were badly hurt. Mephibosheth would never run and play with his friends again. Could anything good ever happen to him now?

If this should happen to a child today, he would probably get well. We have good doctors and hospitals now. But hundreds of years ago they didn't have as many good doctors.

That boy's grandfather, Saul, had been king. But after his grandfather and father were killed in battle, David became the new king. David had been a close friend to this boy's father, Jonathan. One day the new king was thinking about his good friend Jonathan. He remembered that before he

A Lesson in Kindness

ever became king, he and Jonathan had made a promise. They had promised to be kind to each other's children. Wasn't that wonderful for him to think of being kind to his friend's children? You see, every good deed first begins with a good thought.

So what did King David do? He asked for the lame Mephibosheth to come to the palace. But the crippled boy was afraid. He didn't know whether the king wanted to help him or hurt him. He felt so helpless and unimportant. He thought there was no useful place for him in life, because he was a cripple. Thinking this way was actually worse than being crippled in his feet. Success comes from how we feel, not from how well we walk. Thinking we can't do

something will keep us from doing it. If we believe God will use our lives to do good things, good things will happen. Yes, they will, regardless of our looks, size, or health.

Now, the king had sent for the boy and better things were soon to come his way. King David said to him, "Don't be afraid. I will show you kindness, for your father was my best friend. I will give you all the land that once belonged to your grandfather King Saul; and you shall always eat at my table."

Mephibosheth could hardly believe the king's kindness. It was just too good to be true. He asked, "Who am I that you should pay attention to a dead dog like me?"

Should Mephibosheth have called himself a dog, just because he was crippled? Of course not! Sometimes handicapped people can be made to feel like dogs if others do not treat them with respect. But David would not treat anyone like a dog. And neither will we! Now Mephibosheth was still worried that others might think a cripple should not be a guest in the palace. David was not concerned about what other people thought. David knew he was doing right.

When we are truly kind to people who need our help, especially people who are different, we should not worry about what others think. It pleases Jesus for us to be kind to all the people that we know. We should be kind to our parents, brothers and sisters if we have any, classmates, neighbors and other people. Doing kind things for other people will make both them and us happy.

Prayer Thought: Teach me to be kind to everyone I meet.

Let's Talk About the Story:

1. How did Mephibosheth become crippled? If you were Mephibosheth, would you miss being able to run and play?
2. Why did David ask Mephibosheth to come to the palace?
3. Think of a person that you know that you could be kind to. What can you do to help that person?

Mephibosheth

From her arms the little boy fell,
  He was hurt, and couldn't get well.
Though it caused him to be lame,
  God still loved him just the same.
Now God and Jesus love me too,
  So I'll be kind to them and you!

Have you ever made a bird feeder or tossed out some crumbs for the birds?

Usually we feed the birds. But in this story the birds feed the man. This man's name was Elijah. He was a prophet of God. A prophet is one who speaks God's word.

There are different kinds of birds. How many kinds do you know? The birds that fed Elijah were ravens. They were large black birds. They were strong and carried large pieces of food.

The Lord told Elijah to go and hide from some mean people who wanted to kill him. He was to hide by a stream of water that flowed down from the mountains. There Elijah had water to drink. Each morning and evening the ravens brought him food to eat. They brought bread and meat. God had told the birds to take care of Elijah.

But Elijah soon had a problem. It didn't rain for a long time. The streams stopped running and dried up. The Lord knew Elijah had to have water to live. So the Lord told him to go to the town of Zarephath. The Lord told him that a widow there would take care of him.

When Elijah arrived at the town of Zarephath, he saw a woman. She was gathering little sticks for firewood. This was the woman God had chosen to help the prophet. At first Elijah didn't know she was the woman.

Elijah was tired, thirsty, and hungry. So he asked the woman to help him. He said, "Bring me some water that I may drink." Have you ever been really thirsty? Then you know how Elijah felt.

This widow was a good woman. That's why the Lord chose her to care for the prophet. When the Lord wants good things done, He chooses good people to do them. Bad people don't care enough to help.

This widow was kind and good. She went right then to get the water. As she was going, Elijah asked another favor. "Please, I beg you to bring me some bread also."

But the woman didn't have much bread. She answered, "As surely as God lives, I have only a handful of meal and a little oil. I am gathering some sticks to make a fire to cook the meal for me and my son. After eating it, there is no more food. Then we shall starve to death." This was very sad.

But our loving and kind God had another plan. He had the prophet to tell her: "Don't

A Story of God's Love

fear. Do as you are told. First, make me a little cake from the meal and bring it to me, and then you cook some for you and your son. The Lord God says you can take from the barrel of meal, and there will still be as much as ever. Each time you take some meal out, God will put some more in the barrel. And the same will be true of the bottle of oil. God will put more in as fast as you take it out." How would you like a box of cereal or candy like that? There is no way you could eat it all. You take out some and more would take its place.

The woman believed what Elijah said about the meal and oil. She believed so

much that she made the cake of meal for the prophet as he had asked. Then she found there was enough left for herself and her son. There was always meal in the barrel and oil in the bottle. So the prophet, the woman, and the son had food as long as they needed it. This was a miracle. God kept the barrel and the bottle filled. God provided for their needs.

But the story is not over yet. Later they needed God to do some more providing for them. And He did.

The widow's son got very sick and died. Elijah took the boy from his mother's arms and carried him upstairs. Elijah laid the boy on a bed. The first thing he did was pray. Then Elijah stretched himself over the boy

three times. And he prayed again. This was his prayer: "O Lord my God, I pray thee, let this child's soul come into him again."

Can you guess what happened next? Life came back to that boy. He became as strong as ever. Elijah then took him to his mother and said, "See, your son lives."

What a happy way for a story to end. They had their troubles. But God provided for their needs. And all ended well. God who provided for them will also provide for us. May we always trust Him.

Prayer Thought: God, I am so thankful for the way you provide and take care of us.

Let's Talk About the Story:

1. What kind of bird brought food to Elijah?
2. How much food did the widow have in her house?
3. How did God help the widow and her son?

The Widow's Son

She gave the good prophet some bread,
  He raised her dear son from the dead;
So it is nothing new, you see,
  When God takes care of you and me.

Do you know the name of the governor of your state? Who is the president of our country? Both of these people are important. They deserve our respect. We should honor and respect the people God has placed over us for our protection. God has given us parents, teachers, preachers, rulers, policemen and others to help us. When we obey and honor these people, it pleases the Lord. For it makes our world a better place to live.

Hundreds of years ago there lived a Bible prophet named Elisha. He was the person God chose to speak for Him. When a person listened to Elisha's preaching or teaching, he was really listening to the words of God. God expected all of His people to respect and obey Elisha.

One day Elisha was on his way to Bethel. As he was walking along, a group of young boys began making fun of him. "Go on up to Bethel, Baldhead," they jeered at him. Elisha was alone and the boys began closing in on him. How could Elisha protect himself? He called upon God for help.

Would you have felt safe if you had been walking with Elisha that day? Or would you have felt safer inside the group of troublemakers? Would you have had the courage to step away from the crowd and help protect Elisha? Or would you have been too afraid? Would you care more about doing right or would your friends "come first"? God has told us in His Word, the Bible, "Bad friends can cause you to do bad things."

Perhaps you remember a time when someone made fun of you. Has anyone ever laughed at your clothes? Or have you ever fallen down and heard a classmate laugh at you? God loves you just the way you are. He understands that children, and adults too, make mistakes. He accepts the way you look. If you will let Him, He will show you how to use your looks, personality, talents and body to serve Him.

Do you think that being bald kept Elisha from being able to do God's job well? Of course not. Give both your good traits and your weaker ones to God. See what He can do with them!

It is too bad that the young boys in this story did not practice God's Golden Rule. It tells us all to "treat other people the way you want to be treated." If we obey this rule from God, our lives will be happier.

The young people in this Bible story did not think about God's will for their lives. They had to learn a very painful lesson. On that day while they were still poking fun at Elisha, two ferocious bears came out of the woods. The bears snapped, snarled and pawed at the mischievous gang. Forty-two kids in their rowdy group were hurt.

Everyone learned an important lesson: making fun of God and His people is a

2 Kings 2:23-24

serious mistake! Why learn this lesson the hard way — by getting hurt? Or by hurting someone else with careless words that usually end up hurting us more than others?

This story is in the Bible to help us today. Respect God, His people, especially those who teach His Word, and every other human being. Never make fun of anyone! For God loves you and them. And He wants your love and respect in return.

Prayer Thought: Lord, I want to show respect to all people you have placed over me to keep me safe.

Let's Talk About the Story:

1. Who was Elisha? What kind of man was he?
2. Name as many people as you can that the Lord has placed over you to keep you safe and take care of you.
3. Now name some specific ways you can show that you respect these people.
4. Good manners show that you respect others. Name some good manners that you now use or plan to use.

The Young Lads

God's dear Word they had not read,
  Called the prophet, "Old Baldhead"!
Bears came down to get the boys.
  The bears were real — not just toys.

TWO BOYS SAVED FROM SLAVERY

Many years ago in the land of Israel, people's debts could get them in serious trouble. Any person who owed money could be sold, or even his children sold, to pay the debt. Aren't we glad this is not true today?

In one of the homes there was a young father, a prophet, who died. A prophet is a man to whom God spoke. When he died, he left his wife and two precious sons behind. But he left something else — a debt. He owed some money. This could cause trouble for the family. What would they do? The mother could not earn enough money to pay the debt. Women could not get any good paying jobs then.

One day a mean man came to collect the money. He demanded that the mother pay all the money the family owed. She told him, "We don't have any money. We can't pay this debt!" This man, however, was not willing to wait much longer. He said, "I will return a little later. If you don't pay, I will take your two sons and make them my slaves. You either get the money or lose your boys."

This was scary. She loved her boys and didn't want to give them up. There was no way she could make enough money to pay the bill. And she didn't know anyone from whom she could borrow the money. The poor mother didn't know what to do! At last, she thought of the prophet Elisha, a man of God. He had always been kind and helpful to people in trouble.

Sometimes we wait until we are in big trouble before we finally think of God. Sometimes God is the only one who can solve our problems.

So the mother rushed away to see Elisha. She told him, "My husband is dead. He was a good man and served the Lord faithfully. Now we don't have the money to pay the bill we owe. Unless I get the money soon, my two sons are going to be taken away from me and made slaves."

Kind-hearted Elisha wanted to help. He asked, "Tell me, what do you have in your house?"

The sad mother answered, "The only thing I have is a pot of oil."

The prophet Elisha knew that would be enough with God's help. For God could add to it. He said to her, "Go borrow all the vessels — jars, pots, and pans — your neighbors have. Get a lot of them. Take them home and shut the door. Then pour the oil from your pot into the vessels you have borrowed. Fill each of them one by one."

This was a strange bit of advice. Don't you imagine she was expecting money? But Elisha didn't give her money. He told her to pour oil into as many pots as she could find. This command was a strong test of her belief in God.

Did she have enough belief in God to obey? Yes! She didn't argue or complain. She did exactly what she was told to do. And the boys helped her. Now can't you see them running from house to house borrowing pots and pans? After every pot was filled, their own pot of oil was just as full as ever. God added to it and kept it full. She did what the prophet told her, and God helped her. Here is a great lesson for us.

She hurried back to Elisha, the man of God, and thanked him. Then she told him what happened when she did what he told her.

And Elisha said, "Go, sell the oil, and pay your debt. You and your children can live on the money that you have left."

How happy she was! She and her boys could stay together. God had taken care of her needs. Now the mother and her sons could see that God had a plan to save them. As they obeyed in each little step, God made it possible for them to be a safe and happy family again. As we trust God and obey Him, step by step, He will make our lives happy also.

Prayer Thought: Lord, show me many, many ways to obey!

Let's Talk About the Story:
1. Why were the mother and her two sons sad?
2. When the mother asked Elisha for help, what did he tell her to do?
3. Did the mother and her sons obey every step Elisha told them to take?
4. Does trusting in God when you are in trouble make sense?
5. What is the main thing you learned from this story?

Two Boys Saved from Slavery

"Lose your boys if you don't pay!"
  This is what he came to say.
God stepped in and found a way,
  Gave them oil and saved the day.

Have your parents ever warned you not to ride with strangers? They probably would not allow a stranger to spend the night in your home. Your parents feel this way because they want you to be safe.

Long ago in Bible days, people welcomed strangers into their home. The Hebrew people did not have motels or inns. Instead they considered it their duty to offer a traveler a place to sleep in their own home. They didn't have to be afraid of strangers many years ago. Wouldn't it be fun if we could do the same today?

This story is about a special traveler, Elisha, who was a prophet of God. Elisha and his servant, Gehazi, often traveled through the land of Israel. Elisha made these trips to many places. At each place he met with the Lord's people and taught them about God.

One of the little cities Elisha visited was Shunem. In the city was the home of a married couple whose name we do not know. This couple was wealthy and had many servants. But one special joy was missing in their lives — they had no children!

One day the loving woman saw Elisha and his servant, Gehazi. She invited them to her house for dinner. She believed in God and wanted to serve God. One way to serve God is to serve His people. So she tried to make her guests feel very welcome.

From then on, every time Elisha went through Shunem, he ate and slept in this couple's home. After Elisha had come to visit several times, the good lady had an idea. She said to her husband, "This is a ho-ly man of God that passes by so often. Let us build a little room for Elisha on the side of our house. And we can put a bed, a table, a stool, and a candle in the room. Then, whenever Elisha and his servant come this way, they will have a comfortable place to rest."

Her husband liked the idea and worked very hard to build the room. Imagine how delighted Elisha was to see the special room. He knew he was loved and honored.

Isn't it nice when someone gives you a surprise? Sometimes your grandparents give you a gift. When they do, don't you want to do something nice for them? That is exactly how Elisha felt. He wanted to do something really nice for the good Shunammite couple. He said, "You have been so kind that I would like to do something for you in return."

"I have nothing to ask," the woman answered. Remember, she gave to Elisha without expecting anything in return. This was unselfish giving. She did not give to help herself, but to help him.

But Elisha was determined to show his thankfulness. He asked his servant, "What will please the nice woman?" Since the servant knew how important children were to the Hebrew women, he replied, "She has no child."

As a prophet of God Elisha gladly told the woman, "By this time next year you shall have a son." She thought Elisha was teasing. But he wasn't.

The following spring a son was born to the couple. How happy they must have been that God had given them a child! As the boy grew, the Shunammite couple treasured him as a gift from God.

54

One morning when the boy was old enough, he ran into the fields to see his father at work. Suddenly the boy became very sick. He screamed, "Oh my head, my head!"

Immediately a servant carried the boy home to his mother. He was so sick that his mother held him on her lap. But the boy didn't get better. He died! Can't you see her praying, crying, and holding her son so closely?

She sadly carried her dead son to Elisha's room and gently laid him on the bed. Then she called to her servant, "I must hurry to Elisha, the man of God."

She quickly saddled a donkey and rushed about twenty-five miles to Mount Carmel to get Elisha. When she saw him, she fell at his feet. Elisha returned with the broken-hearted mother to her home.

Even when she was sad, the mother kept her faith strong. She didn't give up hope. She asked for help from the man of God.

When Elisha arrived at the couple's home, he went immediately to the room where the

dead boy lay. He prayed for the boy, and the little boy's body changed from cold death to warm life. The boy sneezed seven times and opened his eyes. He was alive again!

Then the boy's mother came back into the room. Imagine her joy! She knelt down at Elisha's feet and bowed herself to the ground. The woman thanked Elisha. But she knew that it was really God who had brought the boy back to life. What an encouraging story of faith!

Prayer Thought: Lord, help me to trust you more.

Let's Talk About the Story:
1. Why did the Shunammite couple invite Elisha into their home?
2. What kindness did the couple do for Elisha?
3. Elisha really wanted to show the couple he appreciated their kindness. What promise did he make?
4. Who really did the miracle in giving life to the dead boy?
5. Is it ever hard for you to trust God? When?

The Shunammite Boy
Out in the fields he said, "My head!"
  He was sick, and then he was dead.
In God they trusted and believed,
  Pain and sorrow He could relieve.
Elisha came, the boy was raised.
  "Glory to God," they gave the praise.

Have you had chicken pox or measles? Remember the ugly sores on your body? Well, this story is about a little girl who helped to cure a man with ugly sores on his body. He had leprosy. Chicken pox soon disappears, but leprosy does not. There is no cure for it. The man who had leprosy was named Naaman. He was a captain in the Syrian army.

One sad day the armies of Syria kidnapped some of God's people from the land of Israel. One of the captives was a young girl. She became a slave in Syria where she helped to take care of Captain Naaman's wife.

Because Naaman had leprosy, he worried a lot. "People might become afraid even to get near me," Naaman moaned. "Who wants to get leprosy? I might even lose my job." But something even worse than that would happen. In time, Naaman knew his leprosy would spread over his whole body. He would surely die!

Should a little Hebrew maid who had been captured, taken to a foreign country and made a slave, care about the captain's problem? What could a little girl so young do anyway? Plenty! She felt sorry for her master. She knew there was a prophet in her land who, through God's help, could heal sick people.

She told Naaman's wife about the prophet. The little girl cared for both Naaman and his wife. Naaman heard this news and excitedly told the king he could find a cure for leprosy in the land of Israel. This pleased the king because Naaman was very valuable to him. The king of Syria said, "Go and I will send a letter to the king of Israel."

So Naaman hurried to Israel. He took many people with him. They carried gifts of gold and silver and changes of clothes. At the palace of the king of Israel, Naaman presented the letter from his own king. The letter said, "Now when this letter is received, the person bringing it is Naaman whom I have sent to you that you may cure him of his leprosy."

The king of Israel was so surprised! He had no cure for this bad disease. "Oh, no!" shrieked the king. "Who does the king of Syria think I am anyway? Can I heal people? He must be trying to find an excuse to pick a fight with me!" The king of Israel tore his clothes and worried!

When the prophet Elisha heard about all this, he sent a message to the king. Elisha said, "Why have you torn your clothes? Let Naaman come to me. You shall know that there is a prophet of God in Israel."

2 Kings 5:1-16

So Naaman went with his horses and chariots and stood in front of Elisha's home. Naaman expected special attention from Elisha. After all, wasn't he Captain Naaman, friend of the king? But Elisha did not go out to see Naaman. He only sent a message: "Just go and wash in the Jordan River seven times and you shall be cured."

"What!" roared Naaman. "The Jordan River is too muddy! There are better rivers in Syria closer to my home! Besides that, I thought the prophet would call on the name of his God and wave his hand over the place and cure my leprosy."

Well, Naaman had some servants who were smarter than he was. They asked him, "If the prophet had told you to do some great thing, wouldn't you have done it? Why not do this simple thing, 'Wash, and be clean?' "

Finally Naaman agreed with the servants and went down to the river. He started dipping. One, two, three, four, five, six times. The seventh time when he came up from the water he was cured!

Now what did Naaman do? He looked down at his skin. It was as fresh and clean as a baby's skin. He shouted, "Now I know that there is only one true God, the God of Israel."

Naaman quickly returned to his home in Syria to share his good news about being healed. But even more important than being healed, he had learned about God. Naaman was so happy, he wanted to tell all his friends about his good news.

All of this happened because of one little girl's love and concern for others. She was the one person who was in the right place, at the right time with the right words to help. Look all around you. Someone may be wanting your help right now.

Prayer Thought: Help me to notice those who are sick and hurting. Help me to show compassion to them.

Let's Talk About the Story:
1. What was wrong with Naaman? Why did he go see God's prophet?
2. How did the little slave girl help make Naaman well?
3. Who really healed Naaman?
4. Name a person you know who is handicapped (crippled, deaf, blind) or sick. How can you help that person this week?

Little Slave Girl

Captain Naaman was a leper,
  His skin was rough you know.
A kindly slave girl told him,
  "To Elisha you must go!"

He went to see the prophet
  Who told him what to do.
He dipped into the river
  And his skin was good as new!

How would you like to be a king or queen? Once an eight-year-old boy became king in the land of Judah. His name was Josiah. His father, Ammon, had been king only two years when the people became unhappy and killed him. Then Josiah, being the oldest son, took his father's place as king.

Though Josiah was king, he looked like other boys. But being king made a difference. He wore the rich, colorful clothes of a king. His crown was made of gold and costly gems. Around his neck and arms were gold bands with expensive pearls in them. His throne was made of gold and ivory. His home was the big, beautiful palace. Around it were flowers and water fountains. He had the best things to eat. Josiah had servants to serve him. He rode in a fine chariot. His servants ran ahead of him and shouted, "The king is coming!" Then the people would stand along the way to see him. As he passed, they would bow to the ground. He was their king!

But being king was not fun all the time. The people had started doing bad things. They had forgotten God. They were worshiping idols instead of God. These idols were made of stone, or iron, or wood. The people talked to them as gods.

Since these people were not worshiping the true God, they became more and more evil. They were not obeying God's laws. They had even lost the Bible. How terrible! And now children were growing up who did not know about God. They did not know God had a book for men and women, boys and girls to follow. The people were living wild and rough lives. They often got drunk, cursed, and cheated. They often got in fights. The Bible meant so little to God's people that they had carelessly lost it.

And now a little eight-year-old boy had been crowned as king of these evil people. At first he was too young to decide what to do. Several older men helped him, especially the high priest named Hilkiah. He taught Josiah the ways of the Lord. As a result, Josiah did what was good in the Lord's sight. He followed God's law exactly without changing it.

When Josiah was eighteen years old, he thought it was time to get rid of the bad things. He commanded that the temple be cleared of all the idols. The temple was dirty and never used. He wanted it to be a place of beauty and purity like it had been. Josiah paid carpenters, bricklayers, painters, and maids to clean it up and repair it. He knew the people needed a good place in which to worship the true God.

As they were cleaning up the temple, guess what they found? Under some old trash they found a strange, rolled-up paper. It was the book of God's law. Many years before this, God had given these words to Moses which he had written on a scroll. Oh, how Josiah enjoyed having the book read to him. He also wanted the people to hear it. Josiah sent messengers throughout the land to call the people to Jerusalem to hear it. When the people gathered, he promised that he would obey God's law and asked them to do the same. They agreed. It was a great day. We should always be glad to hear God's Word.

But the reading of the book also made Josiah very unhappy. It told that God would

punish the people who disobeyed Him. Josiah decided to take action. He sent men throughout the country to break down all the altars and idols.

Many blessings came to God's people. Blessings always come when we read God's Word and follow His way. During the remaining thirteen years of Josiah's life the people were happy and peaceful.

Though Josiah was king, he did not become proud and selfish. He was good and humble and obeyed God.

Josiah proves that if a boy lives where many people are wicked, he does not have to become wicked. Josiah shows that a boy or girl can follow God even when other people do not. Though others may try to make you do something wrong, you can say, "No." You can serve God as Josiah did.

Prayer Thought: Lord, help me to be pure in my life by obeying your Word, not just knowing it.

Let's Talk About the Story:

1. How old was Josiah when he became king? Name some of the good things he did.
2. Name a time when you did the right thing when others were doing the wrong thing.
3. Are you learning Bible verses now so that you can learn to obey God's Word?
4. Do you read the Bible? Do you keep it in a safe place?

Josiah

Young Josiah was his name,
 Being king was not a game,
Loved God's law to the letter,
 Made the land so much better.

An infant boy was once secretly taken out of the palace. He was hidden in a bedroom of the temple. This was done to save him from being killed.

His name was Joash. His father, the king, had been killed. Being a king can be dangerous. Evil people will kill to get to be king, or to get rid of some king they don't like.

After baby Joash's father had been killed, the baby's grandmother, Athaliah, did a terrible thing. She had wicked men to kill all of the dead king's children. This way none of them could take his father's place as king. She wanted to be the queen. She would not share the throne with anyone!

Little Joash, however, escaped the killer's hands. He was lucky to have an aunt who loved him and carried him away to safety. His good-hearted aunt was the wife of the high priest. She and her husband lived in a part of the temple, because he was high priest. She knew that in the temple the killers would not find little Joash. He was safe there.

Now Joash's aunt and uncle were the only ones who knew where he was. It was a hush-hush secret. If Joash had been discovered, his grandmother, Athaliah, would have killed him. So he was hidden for more than six years in the temple. During those years his good-hearted aunt taught him about God, his family, and the duties of a king. She was a good influence on Joash.

All this time, his grandmother was the queen. But the people were becoming unhappy. She was not a good queen. Most

people wanted someone else to be over them. But they were afraid of Athaliah! How could they get rid of her? Who would take her place?

When Joash was seven years old, his life became very exciting. No more hiding. No more secrecy. His uncle, the high priest, decided it was time to let the secret out.

The high priest brought out the little prince and showed him to the people. Joash

A Lesson About Influence

was the rightful heir to the throne. The high priest told the people how the boy's life had been saved. Then Joash was crowned as king. It was thrilling. The people were happy. They blew their trumpets to celebrate. They shouted, "God save the king!"

That wicked grandmother heard all the shouts of joy. She saw the happy people rushing about. She ran to the temple and was she surprised! There was the little prince that she thought had been killed. There he was — King Joash. It angered her. She wanted to be queen. But the people were unhappy with her. They wanted to get rid of her. She was killed outside the temple. Poor Queen Athaliah! Too bad she had not been a sweet, loving grandmother! She had harmed others, and now the harm had come back to her.

As the young king became older, he was helped and guided by his uncle, the high priest. His uncle was a good influence on him.

The boy king began by directing that the temple be repaired. It had been torn down. His grandmother had not used the temple. It meant nothing to her. She had worshiped idols.

For twenty-three years Joash served God. He wanted the people in his kingdom to serve God. Things went well. It was a peaceful and happy kingdom. That is, everything went well until his uncle, the high priest, died.

Now with his uncle's good influence gone, King Joash began to listen to evil people. They gave him bad advice. He forgot about God. Joash became a bad king. The land was filled with misery. His own servants did not like him, and two of them decided to get rid of him. When Joash lay sick on his bed, one of them killed him. How sad!

We see in this story the power of influence. Joash did right in his early life because of the influence of his good aunt and uncle. He later did wrong because of the influence of bad people.

How important it is that you do not follow boys and girls who do wrong. Never repeat ugly words. Never allow them to lead you into doing bad things. Always follow God, and choose to do good.

Prayer Thought: God, help me to choose friends who will influence me to do good things. Help me to be a good influence on others.

Let's Talk About the Story:

1. Who was Athaliah?
2. How was King Joash's life saved?
3. How old was Joash when he was crowned king?
4. What kind of influence did Joash's aunt and uncle have on him?
5. What kind of influence are you on your friends?

Joash

"God save the king," was their cry.
To the queen they said, "Good-bye!"
  Little Joash was the king,
Wore the crown and golden ring.

Be an influence for the good,
You can help your neighborhood.
  Try your best to do what's right,
Be a good friend in God's sight.

Children
of the
New Testament

THE BIRTH OF JESUS

Does your mother or father ever have to take a business trip? Well, Mary and Joseph had to take a trip to Bethlehem to see about their taxes. Bethlehem was about seventy miles from their home in Nazareth. But they didn't go in the car or by plane. There were no cars or planes back then. This was a long way to walk, or ride a donkey or camel.

When they got there, they were very tired. They were looking forward to the comforts of the little hotel. But there was not a room left. The rooms were already taken. Everyone else was paying taxes, too. So they had to stay in the barn. In it they had to make their bed with donkeys, horses, cattle, and camels.

During the night baby Jesus was born to Mary. He was wrapped in soft clothing and laid in a manger for His cradle. A manger is a wooden box or crate that holds hay for the animals. They have to eat, too. The baby was named Jesus which means Savior. God had always planned for Him to save the people from their sins.

The Lord uses people to do things. This means He has something special for every boy and girl to do. Not something as big as He had for Jesus to do. But what God has planned for you to do is important, and He wants you to do it.

Where Jesus was born, hardly seems to us the place for such a great person to be born. He was born in a simple barn. But it caused more excitement than that of any person ever born. A great light shone from

Luke 2:1-20; Matthew 2

the sky on some shepherds. They were watching their sheep on the hills that night. Suddenly angels came and said to the shepherds:

Don't fear; for I bring you happy news of great joy which shall be for all the people. Today in Bethlehem a baby is born — Jesus — who God has planned to save the people. This is how you will know which one He is: you will find a baby wrapped in swaddling clothes, and lying in a manger.

Then many angels sang: "Glory to God in the highest, and on earth peace, good will toward men."

The shepherds then rushed to Bethlehem to find Jesus. Just as the angel had said, they found Jesus in a manger. They dropped to their knees and worshiped Him. Then they went back home and told everybody the wonderful things that happened.

But the shepherds were not the only ones to come and see the child. Wise men from a far-off country also came. One night they saw an unusual star shining in the sky. It was different from other stars. The wise men must have known from the Bible (Numbers 24:17) that a Savior was soon to be born. They rushed away to find Him. The star shone on the road and guided them to the very place where Jesus was. They rejoiced and fell down and worshiped baby Jesus. These men were not only wise but rich. From their riches they gave expensive gifts, each with a meaning. The first gift was gold, a sign that Jesus would be a king. The second was frankincense, which showed that all should worship Him as God's Son. The third gift was myrrh, a sign that He would save us from our sins by dying on the cross.

After Jesus was honored with these presents, an angel of the Lord spoke to Joseph. The angel warned him that baby Jesus was in danger. The angel said, "Arise, and take the young child and His mother, and hurry away into Egypt. You stay there until it is safe to return. For King Herod will look for Jesus and kill Him if he can."

Joseph listened. He took Jesus and Mary, the mother, and left during the night in a hurry.

King Herod had heard about Jesus. He thought Jesus might try to take his place as king. He wanted to be sure Jesus didn't take his place. So he sent men over the country and killed all the boys two years old and younger. He did this mean thing just to kill one baby. He didn't know where to find Jesus. So he decided to kill all the little boys. This way, he would be sure to get rid of Jesus, he thought.

But God was smarter than King Herod. When the baby boys were being killed, Jesus was safe in Egypt with His parents. Let us always remember that God is smarter than anyone — even kings.

After this cruel king died, an angel spoke to Joseph again: "King Herod is dead. Take the young child and his mother and go back home."

Joseph and Mary started back home. Along the way they heard some unhappy news. They learned that Herod's son was the new king. They wondered if the son was cruel and mean like his father. This caused them to change their plans. They decided not to go back to Bethlehem. It might not be safe. For this reason they went to Nazareth instead.

In Nazareth they made their home. There Jesus grew up. There he worked with his father as a carpenter.

Isn't it wonderful that God planned a special baby to save the people and took care of Him? God made you for a reason too, and He will take care of you!

Prayer Thought: Lord, thank you for taking the time to make me so special, the only one just like me. Help me to know what you have planned for me to do.

Let's Talk About the Story:

1. Where was Jesus born?
2. How did the shepherds know Jesus had been born?
3. How did the Wise Men know where to find Jesus?
4. As soon as the Wise Men saw Jesus, what did they do?
5. What did King Herod think of Jesus?
6. How are you unique and special to God?

The Baby Jesus

Jesus came in a humble birth,
  Came to save us here on earth.
The angels sang and Wise Men too,
  "Baby Jesus, we love you."

Have you ever been excited about taking a trip or going on a vacation with your family? Then you know how twelve-year-old Jesus felt when his parents were going to Jerusalem. And to make the journey even more fun, His parents traveled with many of their friends and neighbors. In Jerusalem they celebrated the Passover.

The Passover was a special religious holiday that Jewish families enjoyed once a year. The families thanked God for saving them from slavery in Egypt many years before. Mary and Joseph went to Jerusalem every year. Since Jesus was now twelve years old He was allowed to go for the first time.

After a busy week of activities, the holiday was over. All the friends and neighbors from Jesus' town started walking home. Mary and Joseph went a whole day thinking Jesus was in their group, but He wasn't! As night began to approach, they looked around and Jesus was not there! "Where is Jesus?" they asked. They kept looking, getting more scared and worried all the time. But the boy was nowhere to be found. He was lost!

Finally there was nothing to do but go back to Jerusalem and search there. That's where they last saw Him. Mary and Joseph thought that maybe Jesus was still there, alone, wandering in that big city. They searched everywhere! After three heart-breaking days they looked in the right place, the temple. There Jesus was — safe and unhurt. He was talking about the Scriptures with the Jewish priests and teachers. These teachers of religion were amazed that a boy so young could ask and answer such smart questions.

Suddenly Jesus' parents interrupted everyone. With tears in her eyes, Mary said, "We thought you were lost. We have looked everywhere for you. Why did you treat us this way?" Jesus was sorry His parents were worried. But He was glad He had a chance to learn so much. Jesus had become even wiser. So Jesus answered His mother by saying, "Why were you looking for me? Why, didn't you know that I had to be in my heavenly Father's house learning about His business?"

Jesus was not disobedient to His parents. Never! What He meant was, He must do what His Father in heaven wanted Him to do.

Luke 2:41-52

Now Jesus went back home to Nazareth with His parents and obeyed them. The Bible tells us that people loved Jesus and admired Him. As He grew up, He continued to get more and more wisdom. And Jesus knew where wisdom came from — God! If we want to be wise like Jesus, we will want to learn God's Word. We need to learn it well — just like Jesus did. You are not too young to start right now!

Prayer Thought: Jesus, help me to see the importance of learning: from my parents, at church, and at school. Help me to be wise.

Let's Talk About the Story:

1. Was Jesus excited about going on a trip?
2. Where did Jesus' parents finally find Jesus?
3. When His parents found Him, what was Jesus doing?

The Boy Jesus

They could not find their Jesus,
  It gave their hearts a fright.
Back they went to Jerusalem
  To look with all their might.

Jesus' answer to His mother
  Was so very simple,
When they found Him with the teachers
  Talking in the temple.

THE NOBLEMAN'S SON

A very important official of the king once had a big problem. The son that he loved was very sick. He was about to die!

The boy had a fever. He was getting hotter and hotter. His breathing was getting harder. His mother may have put cold towels on his face and neck and chest. But that didn't help.

Sickness makes people sad. Have you ever been very sick? Being sick can also have some blessings. It brings the members of a family closer together. It causes us to love and appreciate each other more. It makes us give more attention to the sick person. And best of all, it can make us think more about God. It lets us see how much we really need God's help.

This boy's sickness caused his father to see how much they needed Jesus. All other help had failed. The only help left was Jesus. So the father went several miles to find Jesus. He believed Jesus could help his son.

A Story of Jesus' Love

John 4:46-54

The father begged Jesus to go back home with him. That's where the sick boy was. "Sir, please come before my child dies," pleaded the father.

Jesus replied, "Go your way; your son lives." Jesus didn't have to be with the sick boy to heal him. Miles between them didn't stop the Lord's power. This is why the Lord can still help us today even though He is in heaven. The distance between us makes no difference.

The father believed what Jesus said and started on his way back home. As the father was going home, his servants met him. They were so excited! "Your son lives," they said. How happy the father was! The servants told him that his son was cured the very hour that Jesus said the boy would live.

Jesus answered the father's prayer. But Jesus did not do it in the way the father had asked. The father asked Jesus to go home with him and cure his son. Jesus didn't do exactly what the man requested. Jesus had a better way to answer the prayer. He healed the boy right then without going to the father's house.

God will answer our prayers today. He answers them, but not always in the way we ask. Since He is God, He knows the best way to help us.

Isn't it wonderful that we have such a loving and helpful God? This makes it easier for us to be brave. We can sleep in peace every night. We know that He will watch over us and care for us.

Prayer Thought: God, thank you for being so compassionate and loving toward us.

Let's Talk About the Story:

1. Why did the father visit Jesus?
2. Did Jesus care about the father and his sick son?
3. How can being sick help us?
4. Can you think of someone you can help?

A Nobleman's Son

The little boy was so hot
  He couldn't talk or think.
His father ran for Jesus,
  Who healed him in a wink.

THE DAUGHTER OF JAIRUS

Do you know how very much your parents love you? You are so very special to them. They remember very clearly when they first brought you home from the hospital as a tiny baby, when you took your first step, or had your first birthday. They remember when you lost your first tooth, and when you went to school for the first time. Think for just a moment how much your parents love you. Then you can understand why the parents of this twelve-year-old girl were very upset.

The father was a man who believed in God. His name was Jairus. He and his wife and his daughter lived along one of the prettiest streets in a large and important city called Capernaum. It was a busy city, and the streets and shops were alive with people. It was a favorite place. Many people enjoyed living there.

One day Jairus' daughter became very sick. Her parents were very concerned. They gave her the best of care and called the doctors. But she did not get better. Her parents were afraid that she might die!

So Jairus hurried out of his house to find Jesus. After all, Jesus had healed the sick, the deaf, the lame, and the blind. Certainly He could heal a sick girl!

Suddenly Jairus saw a very large crowd. Realizing Jesus must be inside the crowd, Jairus ran even faster. When he found Jesus, he fell down on his knees at the feet of Jesus, pleading, "My little daughter is about to die. Please come and lay your hands on her, so she will get well and live."

Think of the faith Jairus had. He believed that if Jesus just touched his daughter she would not die. So Jesus went with him. Many people followed. They tried to move through the thick crowd of people who wanted to be close to Jesus. But they were stopped by one of Jairus' servants who pushed through the crowd. The servant said, "Your daughter has died. Why trouble the Teacher any more?"

Then Jesus gently put His hand on Jairus' shoulder and comforted him. Jesus said, "Do not be afraid any longer, only believe." So Jairus had faith, just like Jesus wants you to have today. There is nothing too hard for God to do.

Now you can probably guess what happened. When the men arrived at Jairus' home, everyone was crying. Jesus said, "Stop crying; the girl is only sleeping!" The people laughed. They knew better. They knew that she was really dead!

Mark 5:22-43

Jesus took the little girl's hand, and suddenly she stood up and began to walk. Jairus had trusted Jesus and put his faith in Him. Can't you see how excited everyone was? Surely they jumped for joy and hugged each other for a long time.

This story that ended so happily has great meaning for all of us today. For the time will come when Jesus will raise all who have died to live again.

Prayer Thought: Teach me to have faith that Jesus knows what I need in every situation.

Let's Talk About the Story:

1. What happened to the little sick girl?
2. What did Jesus say the girl was doing?
3. What did her father think Jesus could do to help?

The Daughter of Jairus

They all knew that she was dead,
  When they saw her in the bed.
Jesus said, "Now let's not weep.
  She's okay, she's just asleep."
Jesus took her by the hand,
  Gave her back her life again.

THE BOY WITH THE LOAVES AND FISH

A Lesson in Sharing

Matthew 14:14-21; John 6:5-13

Have you ever felt that you were just one small person lost in a crowd? This is a story about a young boy in a crowd of more than five thousand people. Would anyone even notice him? Yes, they would! He was the only one in this large crowd of hungry people who had brought along something to eat. He was a small boy with five barley loaves and two small fish.

But this little boy found out what the Son of God could do with very little. His story is still told today to teach us about sharing even the small things that we have. God can do great things with them.

These thousands of people had gathered on a hillside not far from a big lake. They had come to hear Jesus teach God's Word. Also, they wanted Him to heal their sick loved ones. They were so interested in what was going on that they had forgotten about eating. It was getting late. Soon it would be dark.

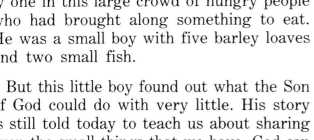

The disciples said to Jesus, "Send the people away so they may get food in the villages as they go home."

But Jesus wanted to feed them before sending them away. He wanted to help the hungry people. Jesus asked Philip, one of His special friends and helpers, "Where shall we buy bread for the people to eat?" He asked this just to test Philip's faith. Jesus already knew what He was going to do.

Philip replied, "We don't have the money to buy enough bread to give each person even a bite to eat."

In the meantime Andrew, another friend of Jesus, had learned something. Andrew found the boy who had something to eat. The boy was willing to share it. But how could such a small amount help such a huge, hungry crowd?

Would you have been willing to share your only lunch with strangers? What if you were at a picnic with your friends and they didn't have enough food to eat? What would you do? Would you run off and gobble your food down? Or would you share it as far as it would go? What do you think Jesus would want you to do?

Well, it made Jesus happy that this good boy was willing to share.

Jesus then asked that this big, big crowd sit down in groups of fifties and hundreds. Why did Jesus do that? He knew that sitting in groups would make it easier for all of the people to be fed. No one would push and shove or be left out.

Now after the people were seated, Jesus gave thanks for the food. Then Jesus gave the bread and the fish to the disciples. They gave enough to every person so that all the people ate until they could eat no more — not even another bite! Thousands were fed with only five loaves and two fish. Jesus had performed a miracle.

Jesus wasn't through yet. He wanted to teach another lesson. He commanded that they go over the grounds and pick up the pieces that were left. They gathered up twelve baskets full of left-over food. This showed that the Lord didn't want anything wasted. Neither does He now.

As the sun went down and the people went home, they kept saying, "It is true that this is the Prophet who should come into the world." The miracle proved it.

Now when everyone left, what do you suppose the boy did? His legs wouldn't run fast enough to take him home! Faster and faster he went. How excited he must have been. For he really had something to tell his mother. He had seen and heard Jesus. He had never before been in such a big crowd. The food he carried had been increased to feed thousands of people.

How happy his mother must have been that her son had a part in such a great event. It made her feel good. Her son had grown into an unselfish, helpful lad. He had given what he had, and Jesus used it and made it bigger. This is why little things given to the Lord's work can become big things.

This boy never forgot the day that he shared his lunch with Jesus and the huge crowd.

Prayer Thought: When I share it makes me happy. Help me to share with others.

Let's Talk About the Story:
1. What miracle did Jesus perform?
2. Imagine what the boy thought when he realized he had something others did not have?
3. If you had been the boy, what would you think after Jesus fed all those people with the food you had brought?
4. Name a way you can share.

A Boy Who Shared

There was a boy who had a lunch,
  Andrew saw him and had a hunch.
Hungry people wanted to eat,
  But their needs they could not meet.
Jesus filled their lunch-time wishes,
  Multiplied the loaves and fishes.

THE LITTLE SICK BOY

Can you remember a time when you were very sick? Your parents were very concerned about you. They love you. They prayed for your good health so you could run and play again.

In this story of a sick boy, his father was very worried, too. His son had a very unusual illness. Nothing that was done to help him did any good. The doctors didn't know what to do to cure him.

The father did everything he could to help his son get well. He tried every cure he heard about. He had heard that Jesus could cure sick people. So he made his way through a large crowd of people and fell to his knees before Jesus.

The father pleaded: "Lord, I have brought unto you my son, my only child. Please help him. He loses control of himself and falls to the ground. Sometimes he even falls into the fire and into the water. When a spell comes upon him, he grinds his teeth, foams at the mouth, and becomes stiff. When he has an attack, it appears that he will die."

Can you see why the father was so upset?

Then the father told Jesus that he had asked the disciples for help, but they couldn't heal the boy.

Mark 9:14-29

It bothered Jesus that His disciples couldn't do anything for the sick child. But He knew why they couldn't. The disciples didn't have enough faith and they had not learned how to pray well.

Soon Jesus would go back to heaven. He wanted the disciples to be able to carry on His work and take care of the people.

Jesus then asked that they bring the boy to Him. And they did. At this very time the boy fell to the ground with one of those attacks and rolled in the dirt. What a terrible sight!

Jesus asked the troubled father, "How long has your son been having these spells?"

The father answered, "Since he was a small child. If you can do anything, have mercy on us and help us."

The man did not need to say "if." But since he did, Jesus used the word "if" also. He said, "If you believe, all things are possible to him that believes."

Immediately the boy's father cried out with tears and said, "Lord, I believe. Help me not to doubt."

Do you know what the loving Jesus did? He commanded that the illness leave that boy. But by this time, the boy was stiff. Many said, "He is dead." Once again the people were wrong and Jesus was right. The kind, gentle Jesus took the boy by the hand and lifted him up. The sick boy was entirely well.

Imagine the boy and his father hugging, kissing, crying, and laughing. What a time to be thankful to the Lord!

Prayer Thought: Lord, teach me to pray when my faith is not strong.

Let's Talk About the Story:

1. What did the father do when he saw Jesus?
2. How did the father describe the boy's illness?
3. Why didn't the disciples help the boy?
4. What did the father in the story realize after Jesus told him all things are possible, if he believed?

A Little Sick Boy

Once, there was a little sick boy,
  His parents were sad, they had no joy.
At Jesus' feet his father fell,
  And Jesus made the little boy well.
When you are sad and full of doubt,
  Believe in Jesus, He'll help you out!

A rose is a very beautiful flower that comes in many different colors — red, white, pink, coral, yellow, and many other colors. A beautiful girl is like a rose, too. She might have brown hair or blonde or red. She might even be named Rose like Rhoda was. Rhoda means "rose".

We don't know what Rhoda looked like, but we do know that she told the truth. Truth is beautiful just like a rose! No matter what we look like, we can all speak beautiful, truthful words like Rhoda did. Then we will be lovely like a rose. The true words that come from our mouths will be like the perfume of a rose.

But some people do not like to hear the truth, especially if they have to change their way of living. Some of the people living in Jerusalem did not want to hear two of God's preachers, Peter and James. Some people did not believe that Jesus was the Son of God. They certainly did not believe that Jesus was alive again in heaven. They wanted to stop James and Peter from preaching about Jesus.

King Herod wanted to please these people. So he arrested James and Peter and some other Christians. After killing James, he kept Peter in prison. This made the troublemakers happy. But the Christians were very sad! Herod planned to kill Peter, too. What could the Christians do to help him? They met at Mary's house. She was John Mark's mother. They prayed, "Dear Lord, please protect Peter."

Meanwhile, Peter was in prison sleeping soundly with four soldiers guarding him. Peter was chained between two of them. One was on his right side, another on his left side. The other two kept watch outside the prison door. Surely four soldiers and stone walls could keep one prisoner from getting loose. But God is stronger than chains, soldiers, and prison walls. And Peter would not be in jail long!

Suddenly a light shone in the prison. One of God's angels touched Peter and awoke him. The angel said, "Get up quickly." As Peter got up, those chains began to break and fall to the floor without even making a sound.

The angel then led Peter past the guards and through a huge iron gate. That gate opened all by itself. The soldiers never even saw Peter. At first Peter thought surely he was dreaming. Later he knew his getting out of prison was real. He said, "Now I know for sure that the Lord sent His angel and rescued me."

It was good to be free. Where should he go to tell his good news? Peter hurried to the home of Mary. There the Christians were still praying for him. He knocked at the door of the gate.

A young servant girl named Rhoda came to the door. It was night and she couldn't see very well. They didn't have porch lights to turn on back then. But she recognized Peter's voice. Oh, how this thrilled her! She was so excited she forgot to open the door. She ran back into the house and shouted, "Peter is here!"

"You are out of your mind," the disciples told her. Yet little Rhoda did not change her story. She insisted that Peter was at the door and she had heard his voice. Then the disciples said, "It must be his angel." They thought Herod had already killed Peter.

"No, I recognized his voice," she insisted. She knew she was right and wouldn't let them talk her out of it.

Peter kept on knocking. Finally, they ran to the door and let Peter in. They were so excited to see him that Peter had to hush them. Peter then told the group the exciting story of how God had sent His angel to rescue him.

In the morning the guards were shocked. Peter was no longer in prison. Yet no one had seen or heard anything. Herod was very angry, but what could he do? He had fought against God — and lost!

Can't you see Rhoda as a happy girl? She had told the truth. When others did not believe her, she insisted that it was so.

Whether you are at home, in school, or on the playground, always tell the truth — and stick with it.

Prayer Thought: Lord, help me to report things exactly as they happen, never bending the truth.

Let's Talk About the Story:

1. Who was in prison? Why?
2. How did the Lord get Peter out of prison?
3. When Peter went to Mary's house, who went to the door first?
4. When Rhoda told the Christians that Peter was outside, why didn't they believe her?
5. Should the fact that you may get a spanking ever keep you from telling the truth?

Rhoda

Peter was well and now he was free,
  Rhoda heard him
And was full of glee.
She ran back the story to boast,
  But they all thought
She had seen a ghost.

Do you have an uncle you love very much?

There was a boy in Jerusalem who did. His uncle was the famous Apostle Paul. Since the boy's mother was Paul's sister, this made him Paul's nephew. The boy loved his uncle, and the uncle loved his little nephew. The people in a family should love one another and stick together. Every child should be true and faithful to his parents, grandparents, brothers, sisters, cousins, aunts, and uncles.

We don't know how old the boy was. But he was young enough that the officers and priests did not notice him. This let the boy learn some news that saved his Uncle Paul's life.

Uncle Paul was a prisoner in the castle. Why? For no reason except that he had been preaching about Jesus.

Paul was in prison, but his enemies wanted him dead. They were not willing for Paul to have a fair trial based on the laws of the land. They wanted to make their own laws or rules.

These men, more than forty of them, made a promise. They promised they would not eat or drink until they had killed Paul. That shows how angry and mean they were. They had a secret plan. They asked that Paul be sent the next day to the court room. While Paul was on the way, they would jump out from a hiding place and kill him. Were these men brave? What do you think?

But Paul's nephew heard the men talking. He was in a crowd of people and heard their secret plan. He walked around listening but probably acted as if he wasn't hearing. That would be easy to do. He could play with a ball, tie some string or look at a pretty rock. But all that time he kept his ears open.

As soon as the boy heard the plan, he ran to the prison to tell his Uncle Paul. Swifter and swifter he ran. He hurried past the guard and went to Paul's room. Out of breath, he told his uncle of the terrible plot to kill Paul.

Paul then called a soldier and said, "Take this young man to the commander. He has something very important to tell him."

So Paul's nephew and the soldier quickly went. The commander, named Lysias, then took the boy by the hand and led him aside. He didn't want anybody to hear. The boy told him about the forty men who were planning to jump on Paul and kill him.

The commander asked the boy not to tell anybody about the plan. Then Lysias started giving orders in a hurry to protect Paul. He called 470 soldiers to go with Paul. Some of the soldiers rode horses. Some walked along carrying long spears.

That night, Paul was brought out of the castle and put on a horse. Then that small army of 470 men quickly moved down the dark street. Most people were asleep and did not know what was happening.

Imagine how angry the forty mean men became when they learned that they had been tricked! How long do you think they kept their promise not to eat?

Paul escaped with his life because of his little nephew's help. That boy was smart. He was brave. He had courage. Maybe you can be a life saver in your home or school or neighborhood — just like Paul's nephew!

Prayer Thought: Lord, help me to always help the members of my family and to have courage.

Let's Talk About the Story:

1. Where was Paul in this story?
2. Who saved Paul?
3. Describe the plan to kill Paul.
4. What can you do to be brave like Paul's nephew?

Paul's Nephew

Forty men took a vow
    To see Paul dead — and now!
The terrible plot the boy did hear,
    And saved Paul's life without a fear.

THE STORY OF TIMOTHY

2 Timothy 3:14-17

Do you love to read or listen to Bible stories? Are you learning Bible verses to guide and help you to know how God wants you to live?

You will enjoy this story about a boy who did just this very thing. His name was Timothy. His mother's name was Eunice, and his grandmother's name was Lois. They loved God and God's Word. Now you can see why Timothy learned about the Bible when he was very young. His mother and grandmother taught him the laws of their people which were written in the Bible. Then he would repeat the stories of the prophets and kings who lived long ago. It thrilled him that he could remember stories from the Bible. And his mother and grandmother were happy that he was learning God's Word. They were so proud of him!

So Timothy grew into a young man who believed in God. Believing in God and God's Word — the Bible — makes a person lovable, happy, and good. If a person has God's love in his life, it just naturally shows in his face. Timothy's face looked shiny and bright. Knowing God's Word gave him confidence in God and in himself. Timothy's face glowed with happiness. Your face can tell others that you love and trust God, too.

How you feel and act will help you to look either more attractive or less attractive. Timothy's beautiful character showed on his face. People were attracted to him. They knew that Timothy loved God and he was a person that they trusted!

One man who liked Timothy very much was the great Apostle Paul, Timothy and Paul were good friends. It was a fine friendship between an old man and a young boy. Paul was strong and educated. Timothy was young and eager to learn. One man was old and the other young, but it made no difference in their friendship. Neither should it today. The Bible makes people love the same God, so they love each other also. The Bible makes the young older in wisdom and the old younger in heart. That's why Paul and Timothy got along together so well. They respected and needed each other. Timothy learned Paul's wisdom. Paul needed Timothy's energy to help him do his work.

The chances are you have some older friends, too. Older people are usually wiser and smarter than younger people.

Timothy was such a good helper that Paul chose him to travel with him to teach God's Word. Paul was proud of Timothy's work. Timothy learned so much from Paul that he later became a very useful leader in the church.

But Timothy's greatest honor came when Paul wrote him two letters. They are called First Timothy and Second Timothy. Those letters are included in the New Testament. They are short but special and very valuable. We can read them today and learn from them just as Timothy did. God wanted us to have those letters, too! That is why He made them a part of the Bible.

The letters told Timothy several things to obey in serving as a wise church leader. One thing Paul commanded him was, "Be a Christian example in everything you do." Paul knew that the easiest way to lead people is by setting the example for them to follow.

We also should be good examples for other people to follow. Then when others copy us, they will learn how to please God.

Timothy went on to become one of the greatest leaders the church has ever had. As he became older, he looked back on the godly influence of his mother and grandmother. They were the first ones to help him become wise by learning God's Word.

Prayer Thought: Lord, help me to study and learn the Bible to be wise like Timothy.

Let's Talk About the Story:

1. What two people first taught Timothy about the Bible?
2. Because Timothy studied the Bible when he was a child, name one special way God used him when he grew up.
3. Name some of the ways you can study your Bible now.

Timothy

Timothy loved it, every word.
　Nothing like it had he heard.
In his heart it did abide,
　The Bible was his friend and guide.

Being a child is not always easy, is it? Adults tell you where to go, what to do, and when to do it. It seems to you that everyone else is taller than you are and you must "look up" to almost everyone. Sometimes adults are too busy to listen to you when you really want to talk. All too often they say, "Run along now — I'm busy — tell me later." Later never seems to come.

The Bible tells us that Jesus always had time for children. Jesus was always very busy teaching God's Word to large crowds. People followed Him everywhere! But He still "made" time to see children. "Children make up the kingdom of heaven," Jesus told men and women. "You must be eager to learn about God and obey Him, like a child, if you want to be in God's kingdom."

Jesus knew that children didn't make up their minds about what was right or wrong before they even listened to the facts. He knew that children were happy to change their minds if they found out that they were wrong. They wanted to learn about life!

One day Jesus was very busy teaching a crowd of people and even healing anyone sick in the crowd. A group of mothers walked up to Jesus' helpers. "We want Jesus to see our children," they said. Will mothers let just anyone hold their children? Would they wait in a long line to do so? They would for Jesus!

"We're sorry," answered the disciples, "Can't you see that Jesus is busy helping the people? We can't stop Him at His work just to see a few children. He has more important things to do."

This made the mothers and children very sad. For a long time they had planned to touch and see Jesus. Probably some of them had come a long way. "We guess that seeing our children is not as important as what Jesus is doing right now," the sad mother said. But they were wrong. The disciple had really been wrong!

When Jesus saw what was happening, He called the children to Him. He was sorry that the disciples were trying to get rid of them. He said, "Don't keep the little children from coming to me. Bring them to me!"

The kind Jesus then took the children in His arms and loved each one. The sight of the children in the arms of Jesus was beautiful. Some of them may have had colds, dirty faces, or snaggled teeth. But Jesus loved them just the way they were. Jesus smiled when the children wrapped their arms around His neck. He enjoyed having their faces touch His.

When the children left that day, they knew that Jesus really loved and accepted them. They were important to Him. The disciples learned an important lesson, too. Everyone, especially a child, is important to God!

A Lesson in Acceptance

Matthew 18:1-7; 19:13-15

When children grow up to be adults, does Jesus just forget about them because they are no longer small? No! He hopes that adults will still want to love and obey Him, the way they did when they were young. Yes, the kingdom of God is filled with children of all ages!

Prayer Thought: Lord, I thank you for loving me as I am; help me to love and accept other people just the way they are.

Let's Talk About the Story:

1. How did Jesus treat the children?
2. What did Jesus say when the disciples wanted to send the children away?
3. How should you love and accept others?

Jesus and the Children

Jesus loved the little children.
   I'm sure He hugged and kissed each one.
He loves us just the same today,
   And wants us all to be as one.

Children of the Bible

The children of the Bible,
  What fun to read their story,
I've learned about the Bible,
  I've learned about God's glory.

There's Ishmael . . . and Isaac . . .
  And the little slave girl, too . . .
And Joseph and Josiah . . .
  All children like me and you.

The children of the Bible,
  Were exciting — every one!
Some were raised to life again,
  And some saw God's dear Son.

On earth, I've only seen them
  In the pages of this book.
But when we get to heaven,
  I shall get a closer look!